LONE PINE

SUSIE BROWN & MARGARET WARNER

ILLUSTRATED BY
SEBASTIAN CIAFFAGLIONE

December 2008

Lightning flashes. Thunder booms. Wind tears at the branches of an old pine tree that stands alone in the grounds of the Australian War Memorial.

Pine cones lie scattered across the ground.

August 1915

Almost a century earlier, on the far side of the world, pine cones lie scattered across a Turkish hillside. A single tree stands alone on the ridge. The soldiers have cut down all the other trees to cover their trenches. Now they crouch beneath a jumble of branches, nervous and silent, waiting for battle.

Suddenly, rifles crack. Gunfire explodes. Bullets whistle across the summer sky.

The Battle of Lone Pine begins.

The fighting is fierce. Many soldiers are killed.

When the battle is over, pine cones lie crushed on the rocky ground. A young Australian soldier moves cautiously across the ravaged hillside. Broken branches snap beneath his boots as he searches for his younger brother.

He hopes his brother is still alive.

The soldier looks down. He stoops and plucks a pine cone that is still clinging to a branch. Holding it up, he breathes in the fresh clean scent of pine. He thinks of his mother's garden where he used to play with his brothers.

The soldier slips the pine cone into his pocket. It is a reminder of this sad day.

Then he keeps searching for his brother.

In an Australian town, an anxious mother waits beside the letterbox. News from the battlefields takes weeks, sometimes months, to reach where she lives.

At last, a parcel arrives. The mother recognises the handwriting and her heart skips a beat.

Carefully, she unties the string and folds back the brown paper.

Inside the parcel is a pine cone.

She holds it up. Its scales feel rough against her fingers. She inhales the scent of distant places, and she knows that her son once held this same cone in the palm of his hand.

Gently, she slips the pine cone into a drawer, where it will stay safe.

The pine cone lies in the drawer, not quite remembered, not quite forgotten.

One day, the mother opens the drawer.

She picks up the pine cone and thinks of her three soldier sons.

Two have returned but her youngest never will.

As she turns the pine cone around in her fingers, several pale brown seeds float down to the floor.

She gathers the seeds and plants them in a pot. She places the pot in a sheltered part of her garden, where the seeds will be warm in the sun and protected from the wind.

Each time she waters them, she thinks of a solitary pine tree on a faraway hillside.

One morning, a few weeks later, the first tender green shoots appear. Before long, three saplings start to grow, their stems reaching for the sun.

Two of them grow sturdy and strong.

But the needles on the third sapling turn brown. They wither and drop to the ground.

The third sapling does not survive.

The other two saplings grow taller. Their branches are sturdy, their needles are glossy and green.

It is time to plant them where they will remind people of the Battle of Lone Pine and the soldiers who died there.

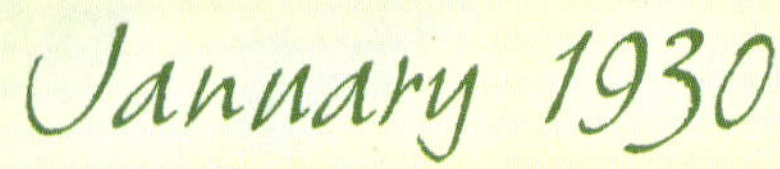

January 1930

The soldiers' mother takes one of the trees to the railway station and sends it to Inverell, the town where her sons grew up. A few days later, the people watch as a gardener plants her tree in the town's main park.

Then they place a plaque at its base in
remembrance of her son who died.

She sends the second tree to Canberra. Another gardener watches over the tree in the nursery while a war memorial is being planned.

The soldiers' mother writes often
to ask how her tree is growing.

October 1934

On a warm spring day, the Duke of Gloucester plants the tree in the grounds of the Australian War Memorial.

That afternoon, the sky turns dark. Lightning flashes, thunder booms.

Wind tears at the branches of the young pine tree.

At last the sky clears.

The years pass.

The tree weathers many storms ...

but the Lone Pine still stands proud and strong.

Lest we forget.

Real people and events inspired this story.

The battle

The Battle of Lone Pine was fought between Turkish and Australian soldiers from 6 to 9 August 1915, on a section of the Gallipoli Peninsula known as '400 plateau'. After three days of fighting, thousands of soldiers had been killed. Seven Victoria Crosses, the highest award for bravery, were later awarded to Australian soldiers.

The trees

The Canberra tree survived the storm in 2008. Commemorative items such as brooches, small boxes and pens have been made from the fallen branches.

In August 2007, the Inverell tree was cut down due to disease. A young tree grown from its seed was planted in its place. On 6 August 2008, Benjamin's son, Allan Smith, planted a Lone Pine tree in the grounds of Inverell High School.

Many new trees have been grown from seeds collected from pine cones at Canberra and Inverell. In 1990, a group of Anzac veterans returned to the Gallipoli peninsula with two of these trees, which were planted during a special ceremony. Trees continue to be planted in memorial gardens and school grounds all over Australia.

The mother

Jane Pyne Perry married James Smith in 1881. She lived in the area around Inverell, NSW, and raised six sons: Thomas, James, William, twins Benjamin and Bertered, and Mark. Later, she married George McMullen and moved to Cardiff, NSW, where she grew the Lone Pine trees. An experienced gardener, Jane was known for her green thumbs.

The soldiers

Benjamin Smith enlisted in August 1914, when he was 25 years old. He was a member of the 3rd Battalion, which was involved in both the landing at Gallipoli and the Battle of Lone Pine. He later fought in France in 1917. He returned to Australia in early 1918 and lived in Inverell.

Mark Smith enlisted as Mark Drice in September 1914, aged 21. He was a member of the 4th Battalion, which was also involved in both the landing at Gallipoli and the Battle of Lone Pine. Mark died sometime during the Battle of Lone Pine. It is unknown whether Benjamin ever found Mark's body on the battlefield.

Benjamin's twin brother, **Bertered Smith**, enlisted in 1916, aged 27. He fought with the 3rd Machine Gun Battalion at Passchendaele and the Somme. He returned to Australia in 1919 and was awarded the Military Medal for 'conspicuous courage and devotion to duty'.

This story is dedicated to the soldiers who fought at Lone Pine and to their families who loved them—SB & MW

For Mum—SC

Hardie Grant acknowledges the Traditional Owners of the Country on which we work, the Wurundjeri People of the Kulin Nation and the Gadigal People of the Eora Nation, and recognises their continuing connection to the land, waters and culture. We pay our respects to their Elders past and present.

Little Hare Books
an imprint of Hardie Grant Children's Publishing
Wurundjeri Country
Level 11, 36 Wellington Street
Collingwood VIC 3066
Melbourne | Sydney | San Francisco

hardiegrant.com/childrens

ISBN: 9781761216114
First published 2012
This edition published 2025

A catalogue record for this book is available from the National Library of Australia

Design Vida and Luke Kelly with Hannah Janzen
Printed in China by Leo Paper Group

The paper this book is printed on is from FSC®-certified forests and other sources. FSC® promotes environmentally responsible, socially beneficial and economically viable management of the world's forests.

2 4 5 3 1